PIRATES

# PIRATE'S LIFE

BY JOHN ABDO

**Fly!**
An Imprint of Abdo Zoom
abdobooks.com

## abdobooks.com

Published by Abdo Zoom, a division of ABDO, P.O. Box 398166, Minneapolis, Minnesota 55439. Copyright © 2022 by Abdo Consulting Group, Inc. International copyrights reserved in all countries. No part of this book may be reproduced in any form without written permission from the publisher. Fly!™ is a trademark and logo of Abdo Zoom.

Printed in the United States of America, North Mankato, Minnesota.
102021
012022

THIS BOOK CONTAINS
RECYCLED MATERIALS

Photo Credits: Alamy, Granger Collection, iStock, Shutterstock
Production Contributors: Kenny Abdo, Jennie Forsberg, Grace Hansen
Design Contributors: Candice Keimig, Neil Klinepier, Laura Graphenteen

Library of Congress Control Number: 2021940193

## Publisher's Cataloging-in-Publication Data

Names: Abdo, Kenny, author.
Title: Pirate's life / by Kenny Abdo
Description: Minneapolis, Minnesota : Abdo Zoom, 2022 | Series: Pirates |
    Includes online resources and index.
Identifiers: ISBN 9781098226909 (lib. bdg.) | ISBN 9781644947050 (pbk.) |
    ISBN 9781098227746 (ebook) | ISBN 9781098228163 (Read-to-Me ebook)
Subjects: LCSH: Pirates--Juvenile literature. | Pirates--History--Juvenile literature. |
    Piracy--Juvenile literature.
Classification: DDC 910.4--dc23

# TABLE OF CONTENTS

# PIRATE'S LIFE

If being on the sea, fighting battles, and stealing treasure excites your imagination, then the pirate's life is for thee!

From sleeping to eating and **plundering** treasures, there's plenty to dig up about a pirate's life!

# YE OLDE YARN

Pirates were thieves, and sometimes violent criminals, who sailed the open waters of the world.

The first documented pirates may have come from the **Aegean Sea** in the Mediterranean more than 2,000 years ago. They were called the Sea Peoples.

Since people have sailed the seas, there have also been criminals who wanted to take things by force. Pirates started out as sailors. They learned that stealing was the quickest way to make a living.

# VAST BOUNTY

A pirate's main bounty was food and supplies for sailing. Pirates had no problem pillaging villages when in need. Riches like gold and jewels were just a bonus.

13

Captains usually rested in private, **luxury** sleeping quarters. The rest of the mates bunked in a small open space with dozens of other crew members.

The preferred bed in a pirate ship was a hammock. It would rock and sway with the ship's motions, providing a good night's sleep. While awake, pirates needed to eat!

Some pirate food favorites were salted meat, **sea biscuits**, and bone soup. Pirates did not do much fishing, so seafood was rare. However, they would steal **livestock** and keep it on board.

Fresh water on board was used for drinking, not bathing. Men lowered themselves into the ocean to cool off but not to be clean. Lack of cleanliness and poor diet led to diseases like **scurvy** and **dysentery**.

Pirates also had to maintain their ships. This meant cleaning and making repairs so the ships could sail on. Stolen goods were used as currency to pay for ship repairs.

Pirates loved to eat, laugh, and be merry! They loved benefits of pirate life. Each celebration was important to them because they didn't know if it would be their last.

The life of a pirate wasn't always fun and exciting. But for the buccaneers who lived to tell the tale, it was truly a treasure.

# GLOSSARY

**Aegean Sea** – a body of water that lies between the coasts of Greece and Asia.

**dysentery** – a common and fatal disease among pirates where the intestines of the victims would swell.

**livestock** – a group of farm animals raised to produce food to eat.

**luxury** – something extremely comfortable and extravagant.

**plunder** – to steal goods and other things through violence and dishonesty.

**scurvy** – a common disease among sailors and pirates. It was caused by lack of vitamin C.

**sea biscuits** – also known as hardtack, hard biscuits that were able to be stored on ships for very long periods of time.

# ONLINE RESOURCES

**Booklinks**
**NONFICTION NETWORK**
FREE! ONLINE NONFICTION RESOURCES

To learn more about a Pirate's Life, please visit **abdobooklinks.com** or scan this QR code. These links are routinely monitored and updated to provide the most current information available.

# INDEX